B~OOKEE~ & L~A~ L~A~

WORDS OF

WISDOM

"Don't just let life happen to you,

happen to life."

Dr. Shawn Council, Esquire, LPD

Introduction

Life lessons are meant to affirm and encourage children everywhere to enjoy school, exercise, help out at home, and develop a healthy attitude about themselves and their respective communities.

Dr. Shawn Council, Esquire, LPD

Contributors and Dedication

This work would not have been possible
without the contributions of

Young Studios, Illustrator.

*This book is dedicated to all of the Bookee(s)
and La La(s) in the world.
You matter.*

Bookee, why is the water running from the fire hydrant? Who did this? We must take care of our neighborhood.   The water cost a lot of money and it is just wasting on the sidewalk

for no good reason.

We must call the Fire Department and ask it to come here and turn it off right away.

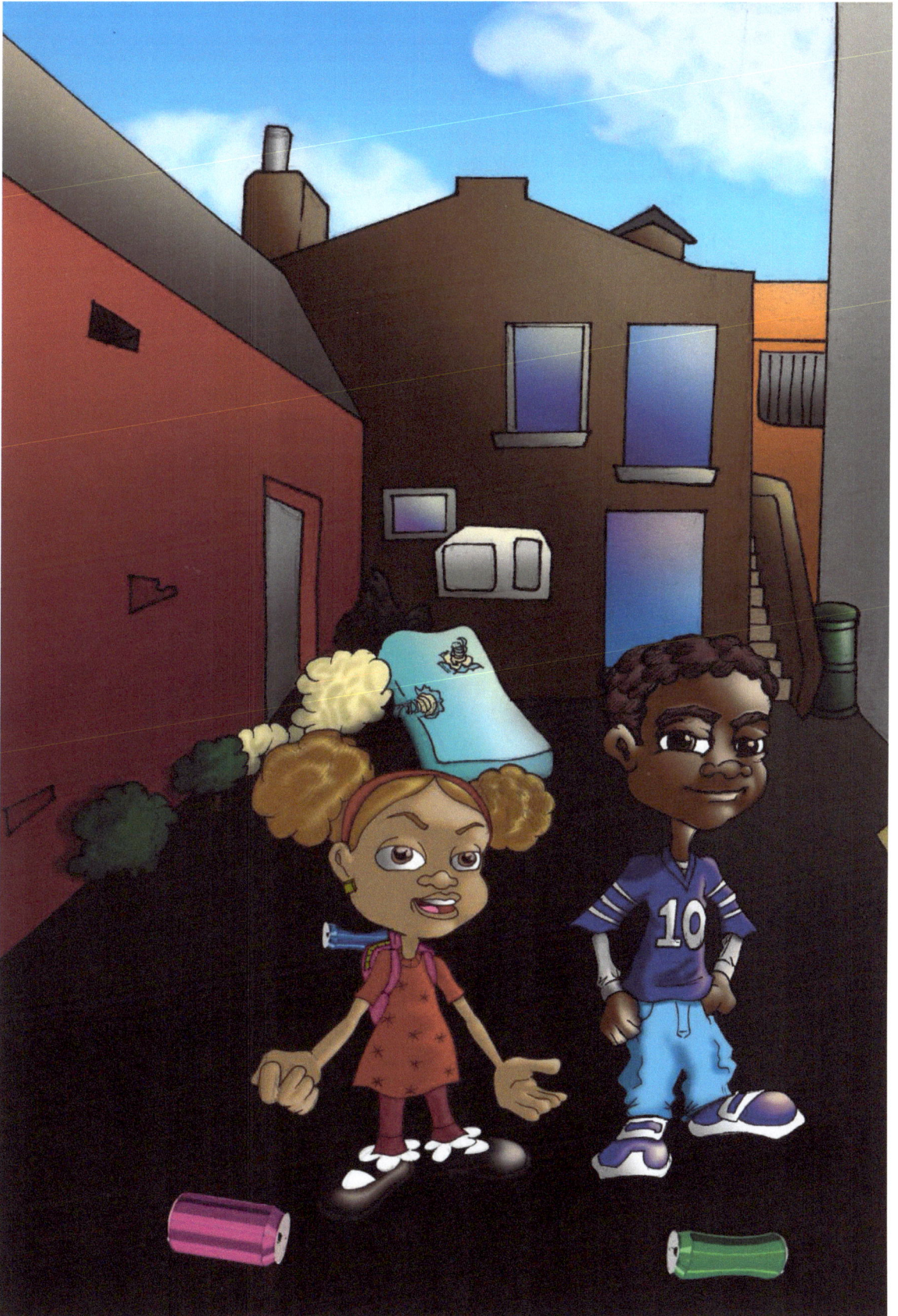

Bookee, trash is everywhere! Why don't people put trash in the trash can? We have to keep our neighborhood beautiful and squeaky clean.

Let's pick this trash up right now!

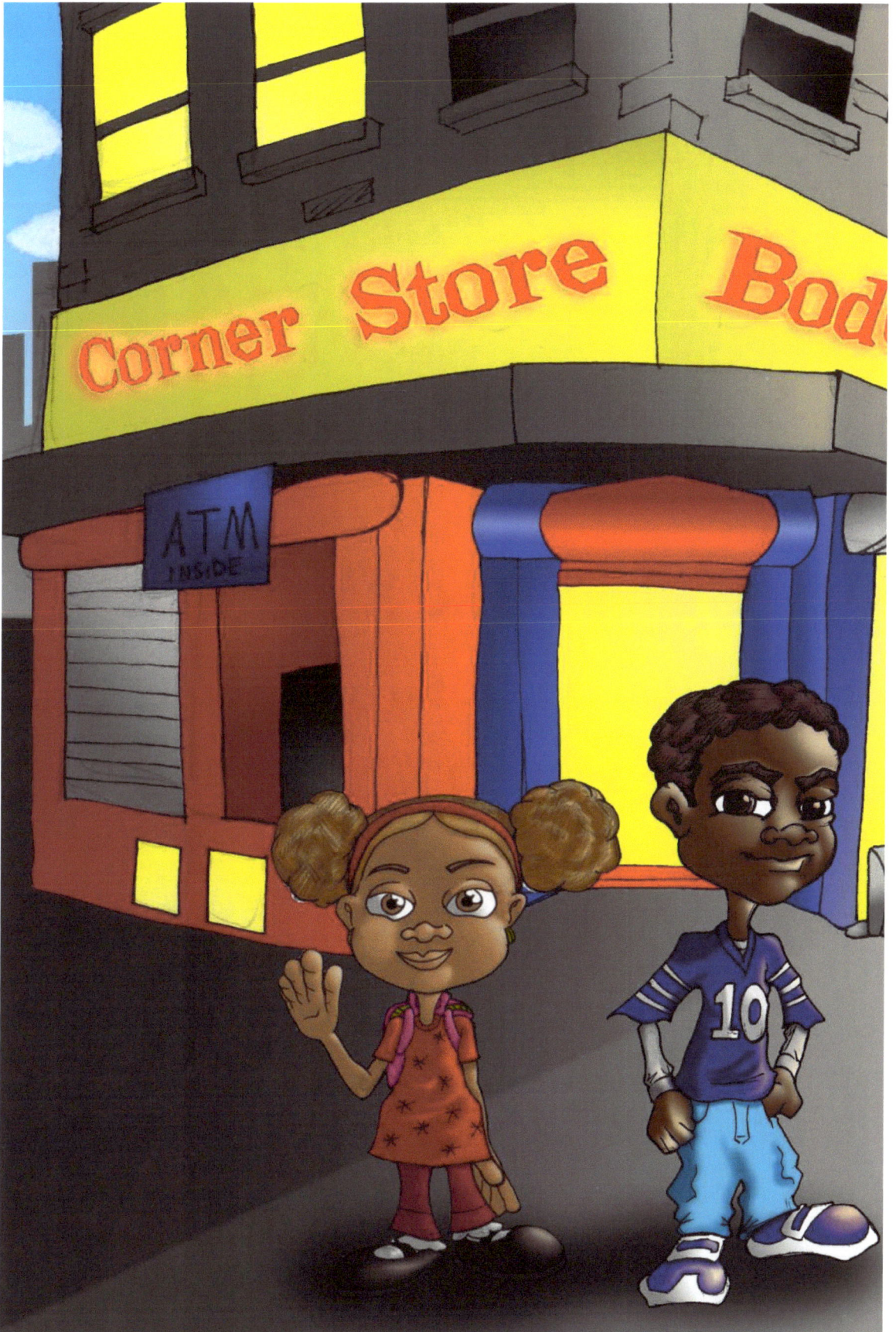

Bookee, guess what? I really like this little grocery store. The owner always has fresh fruits and vegetables for us to buy. The owner is so nice. We need more businesses in our neighborhood. When I grow up, I am going to start a business here in our neighborhood too.

6

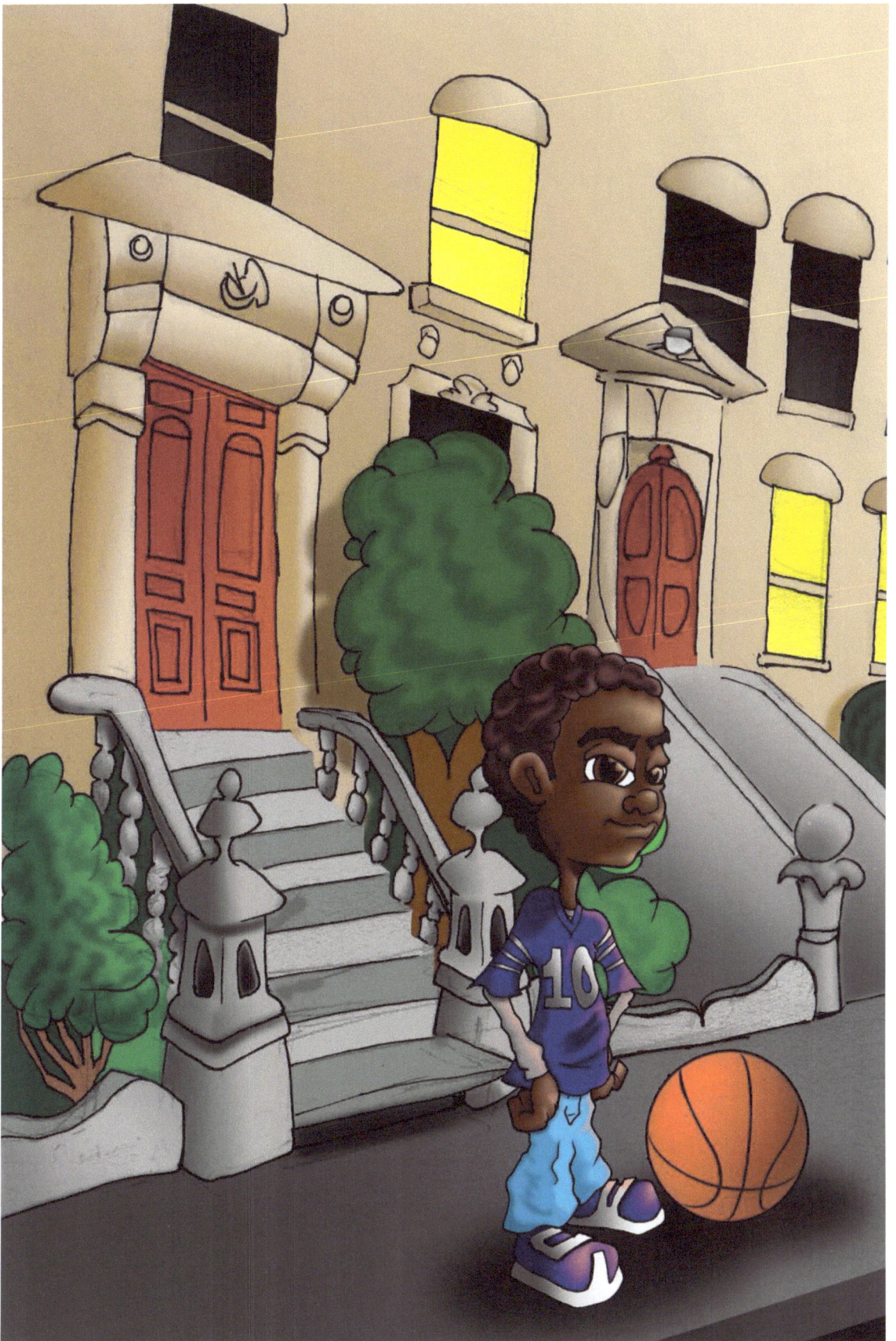

I am all alone, with no one to play with me. My Dad hasn't come to see me for awhile. Where is he and why is my mother so sad all of the time? Mom works a lot and when she comes home,

she is very tired.

Maybe I should go inside and do my homework, after I shoot a few hoops for exercise. When my mother gets home, I will ask her if we can call my Dad and invite him over to play with me this weekend.

It is important for me to see my Dad too...

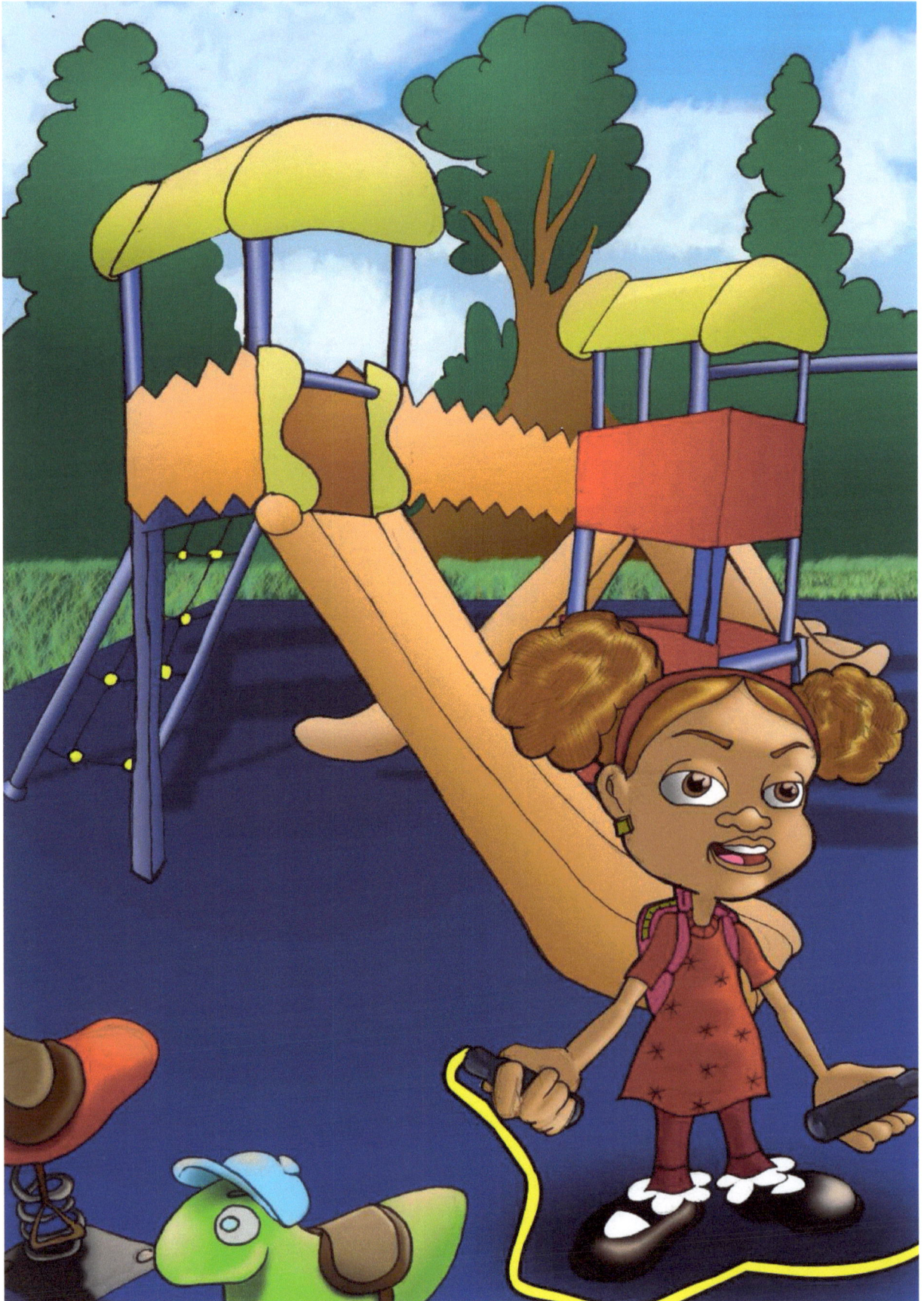

The fresh air and exercise feels good. I love to swing, jump rope, run in the park and ride my bicycle. Where are my roller-skates? I bet I can skate around the whole block in less than an hour...

I must find them.

Hi, La La. How was school today? Let's sit at the kitchen table and do our homework before Mom comes home and starts cooking dinner.

Do you want half of my apple?

I love school because it makes me smart. School is good because it will get me ready for a good future. When I grow up, I can be a Doctor, a Nurse, a Lawyer, an Engineer, a Physical Therapist, a Teacher or a Professor. The list is endless. I can be whatever I want to be. Bookee can even be the President of the United States of America. Hey, I can be the President of the United States too.

I will go to college and graduate with a degree.

I will always learn new things because

learning is fun.

School is fun.

Being smart is fun too.

I know the answers to the questions because I read my book and completed my homework. Sometimes, the other kids laugh at me when I raise my hand to answer the teacher's questions. I ignore them and imagine that they are invisible. I am going to school to learn and

I am responsible for my education.

I have the ability to excel in school.

I am a smart and life-long student.

I am mad at the world. Nothing goes my way. What can I do differently? I need to get a good education so that I can

make my community better.

But first, I have to get rid of some of this anger. Maybe if I exercise and find something that I can do well, I will feel better about myself. I know I have to

get myself together.

The guys on the corner are always trying to get me to go with them but I refuse. I don't need to hang-out with them because they are always getting into trouble.

Wherever they are, the police soon follow. I don't want that life. So, I better get happy about going to school.

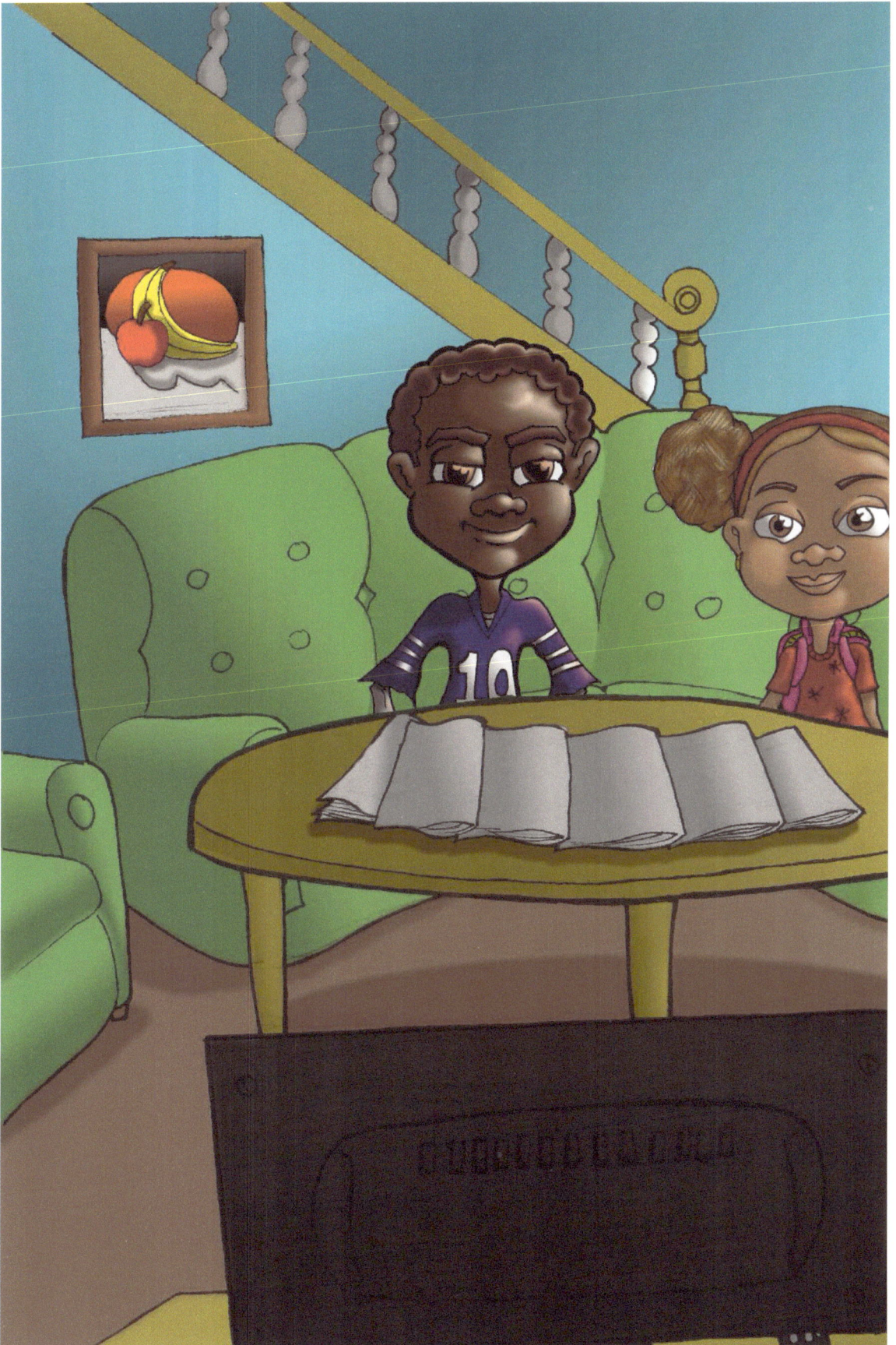

Well, we finished our homework a few minutes ago. Let's watch a little TV until Mom gets home. Then we can help her cook dinner.   But before we watch TV, let's quiz each other on what we learned in school today.

Alright La La? Sure Bookee, you go first.

The End.

ABOUT THE AUTHOR

Dr. Shawn Council, Esquire, LPD is a practicing attorney in Connecticut. She has handled thousands of family related matters. She is also a Professor of Philosophy, Social Justice and African American Studies at Central Connecticut State University. She received her B.A. from the University of California at Los Angeles, a J.D. from The University of Houston and a Doctorate in Law & Policy from Northeastern University in Boston, MA.

www.ingramcontent.com/pod-product-compliance
Lightning Source LLC
Chambersburg PA
CBHW042117040426

42449CB00002B/83